FAVORITE PIANO CLASSICS

83 BEST-LOVED WORKS

EDITED BY

Ronald Herder

DOVER PUBLICATIONS, INC.
Mineola, New York

Bibliographical Note

This Dover edition, first published in 1996, is a new compilation of music originally published in earlier Dover editions and other authoritative publications. This edition adds a few missing tempo markings and dynamics (shown in square brackets), and deletes editorial changes thought not to be original with the composer—especially all fingerings and pedalings incorporated by later editors as well as excessive markings for dynamics and phrasing.

The composer's name in a main heading is always followed by the name of his or her native country. Where two countries are named, the second refers to one closely identified with the composer's career.

International Standard Book Number: 0-486-29152-9

Manufactured in the United States of America
Dover Publications, Inc., 31 East 2nd Street, Mineola, N.Y. 11501

CONTENTS

Titles are given in the language most closely associated with them.

ALPHABETICAL LIST OF TITLES

GLOSSARY OF TEMPO INDICATIONS

French, German and Italian tempo words in this edition

adagio (sostenuto), very slow (and sustained)
agitato, agitated, excited
alla marcia e molto marcato, in march tempo
    and very accented
allarg[ando] (sempre), slowing down (always)
allegretto, moderately fast
    grazioso, moderately fast, with a graceful lilt
    tranquillo, moderately fast and tranquilly
allegro, fast
    con brio, fast, with vigor and spirit
    giusto, fast and in strict time
    marziale, fast and martial
    moderato, moderately fast
    non troppo, not too fast
    vivace, fast and lively
andante, walking tempo
    con moto, walking tempo, moving along
    grazioso, walking tempo, with a graceful lilt
    très expressif, walking tempo, with a very
        expressive feeling
andantino (molto cantabile e con dolore), slightly faster
    than a walking tempo (and very songful and sad)
and^{no} = *andantino*
andantino quasi allegretto, faster than *andantino*,
    almost *allegretto*
animé, animated, lively
assez doux, mais d'une sonorité large, rather gentle,
    but with a full tone
a tempo (I°) [1ᵉ Mouvᵗ], return to the first
    [*primo, première*] speed
    più lento, return to the first speed but a bit
        slower than before
    poco animando, return to the first speed but
        slightly livelier than before

ben moderato, senza rigore e sempre tempo rubato,
    rather moderate, without strictness and
    always with a flexible give-and-take tempo

calmato, calmed
cédez, hold back, restrain the forward motion

con moto, with motion, quick
con spirito, spiritedly

en animant, moving along
en élargissant (beaucoup), broadening (a great deal)
en mesure, in time

frisch und munter, bright and gay

in tempo, return to the first speed

largamente / large, broad, full
largo, very slow, stately
lent (et douloureux), slow (and mournful)
lento, slow
    (ma) non troppo, slow but not too much so
    placido, slow, in a peaceful manner
lunga, long [refers to the length of a held note
    (fermata) in the music]

moderato, moderately
    comodo assai e con delicatezza, moderately,
        very easy-going and with delicacy
    non tanto, pesantemente, not so moderately,
        weighty
molto più lento capriccio, somewhat slow, but played
    very freely
molto vivace, very fast and lively
morendo jusqu'à la fin, dying away until the end
mosso, with motion
mouvᵗ, 1ᵉʳ, first (original) tempo

non presto, ma a tempo di ballo, not fast,
    but in dance tempo

perdendosi, dying away [in speed and volume]
più, more
    all° [allegro], faster
    animato con passione, livelier, passionately
    lento, slower
    mosso, faster
    vivo, livelier

poco, a little, somewhat
   allegretto, a bit slower than *allegretto*
   allegro, con affetto, a little fast,
     with warm feelings
   animato con passione, more animated,
     and passionate
   lento e grazioso, somewhat slow and graceful
   moto, a little motion (movement)
   rit[ardando], slowing down a little
   riten[uto], holding back a little
   rubato, with some flexible give-and-take
     in the tempo
   scherzando, somewhat lightly and playfully
   string[endo], rushing forward a little
presto, very fast

quasi lento e smorzando, almost slow and dying away

rall[entando], slowing down
rapidamente, rapidly
reprenez le mouvement, resume the previous tempo
retenu, held back
rit[ardando], holding back (gradual tempo change)
riten[uto], held back (immediate tempo change)
rubato, a flexible give-and-take in the tempo

scherzando, lightly, playfully
scherzoso, playful, jesting

sempre, always
senza, without
slentando, slowing down
smorzando, fading away in tempo and volume
sostenuto, sustained
stretto, gathering force, accumulating energy
stringendo (sempre), hurrying (always)
subitement, suddenly

tempo, time, beat speed
   di marcia, in march tempo
   di mazurka, in mazurka tempo
   di valse, in waltz tempo
   primo (I°), first (original) tempo
   rubato (un peu moins vite), a flexible give-and-take
     in the tempo (not quite so fast)
toujours (retenu), always (held back)

un peu, a little
   moins vite, not quite so fast
   plus lent, a little slower
   retenu, somewhat held back
un poco mosso, a little more

vif, briskly
vivace, vivace, lively
vivo, quick, lively

FAVORITE
PIANO CLASSICS

Tango in D Major
Op. 165, No. 2
(From *Six Album Leaves*, 1890)

Isaac Albéniz
(Spain, 1860–1909)

Two Minuets in G Major

(From *The Little Notebook for Anna Magdalena Bach, ca.* 1722)

Minuet I

Johann Sebastian Bach
(Germany, 1685–1750)

[Andante grazioso]

Minuet II

[Andante grazioso]

Prelude No. 1 in C Major

(From *The Well-Tempered Clavier*, Book I, 1722)

Johann Sebastian Bach

Invention No. 1 in C Major

(From *Fifteen [Two-Part] Inventions*, 1723)

Johann Sebastian Bach

Invention No. 8 in F Major

(From *Fifteen [Two-Part] Inventions*, 1723)

Johann Sebastian Bach

The Maiden's Prayer

(1856)

Andante

Tekla Bądarzewska-Baranowska
(Poland, 1834–1861)

Bagatelle: "Für Elise"

(1808)

Ludwig van Beethoven
(Germany & Austria, 1770–1827)

Minuet in G Major

(ca. 1795)

Ludwig van Beethoven

Men. da capo.

Minuet in E-flat Major

(ca. 1795)

Ludwig van Beethoven

[Poco allegretto]

"Moonlight" Sonata
Op. 27, No. 2
(1st Movement of *Sonata quasi una Fantasia*, 1801)

Ludwig van Beethoven

marcato, ma sempre *p*

Four Waltzes

(From *Waltzes*, Op. 39, 1865)

Johannes Brahms
(Germany & Austria, 1833–1897)

15

Hungarian Dance No. 5

(Arranged by the composer, 1872, from the original for piano four-hands)

Johannes Brahms

Mélancolie

(No. 2 from *Pièces Pittoresques*, 1880)

Emmanuel Chabrier
(France, 1841–1894)

Scarf Dance

(Arrangement of the Air from the ballet *Callirhoë*, 1888)

Cécile Chaminade
(France, 1857–1944)

Prelude in E Minor

Op. 28, No. 4

(From *24 Préludes*, 1836–9)

Frédéric Chopin
(Poland & France, 1810–1849)

Prelude in A Major
Op. 28, No. 7

Frédéric Chopin

Prelude in C Minor
Op. 28, No. 20

Prelude in D-flat Major ("Raindrop")
Op. 28, No. 15

Frédéric Chopin

"Minute" Waltz in D-flat Major

Op. 64, No. 1

(From *Three Waltzes*, 1846–7)

Frédéric Chopin

Mazurka in A Minor
Op. 17, No. 4
(From *Four Mazurkas*, 1832–3)

Frédéric Chopin

Polonaise in A Major ("Militaire")
Op. 40, No. 1
(From *Two Polonaises*, 1838–9)

Frédéric Chopin

Allegro con brio

Nocturne in E-flat Major

Op. 9, No. 2

(From *Three Nocturnes*, 1830–31)

Frédéric Chopin

First Arabesque

(From *Two Arabesques*, 1888–91)

Claude Debussy
(France, 1862–1918)

Tempo rubato (un peu moins vite)

Clair de Lune

(From *Suite Bergamasque*, 1890, revised 1905)

Claude Debussy

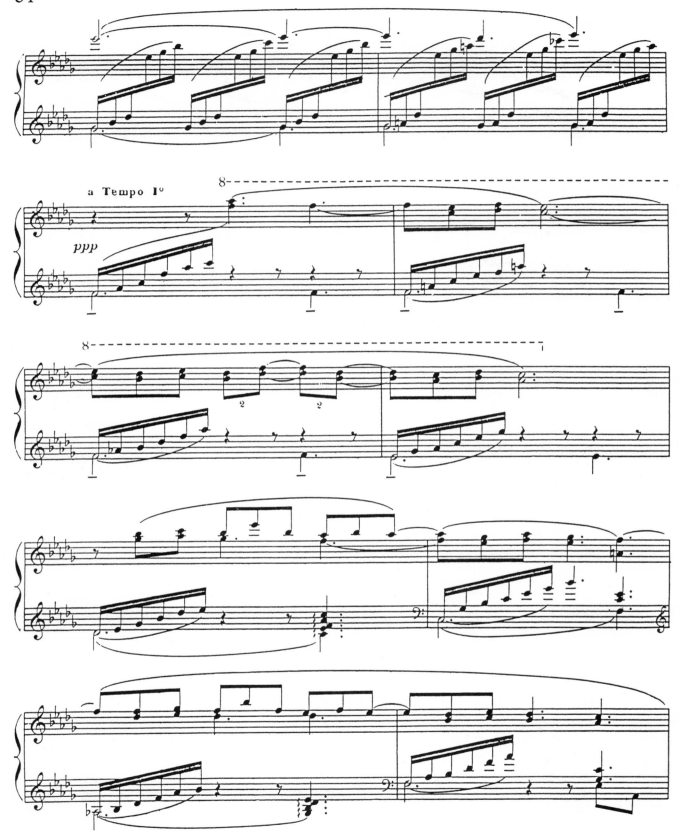

Golliwogg's Cake Walk

(From the suite *Children's Corner*, 1906–8)

Claude Debussy

68

Humoresque in G-flat Major
Op. 101, No. 7
(From eight *Humoresques*, 1894)

Antonín Dvořák
(Czechoslovakia, 1841–1904)

Salut d'Amour

[Love's Greeting] Op. 12 (1888)

Edward Elgar
(England, 1857–1934)

Ballet Air

(Arranged from the opera *Orfeo ed Euridice*, 1762)

Christoph Willibald Gluck
(Austria, 1714–1787)

Spanish Dance No. 5 in E Minor

(From *Ten Spanish Dances, 1892–1900*)

Enrique Granados
(Spain, 1867–1916)

Notturno

[Nocturne] Op. 54, No. 4

(From *Lyric Pieces*, 1891)

Edvard Grieg
(Norway, 1843–1907)

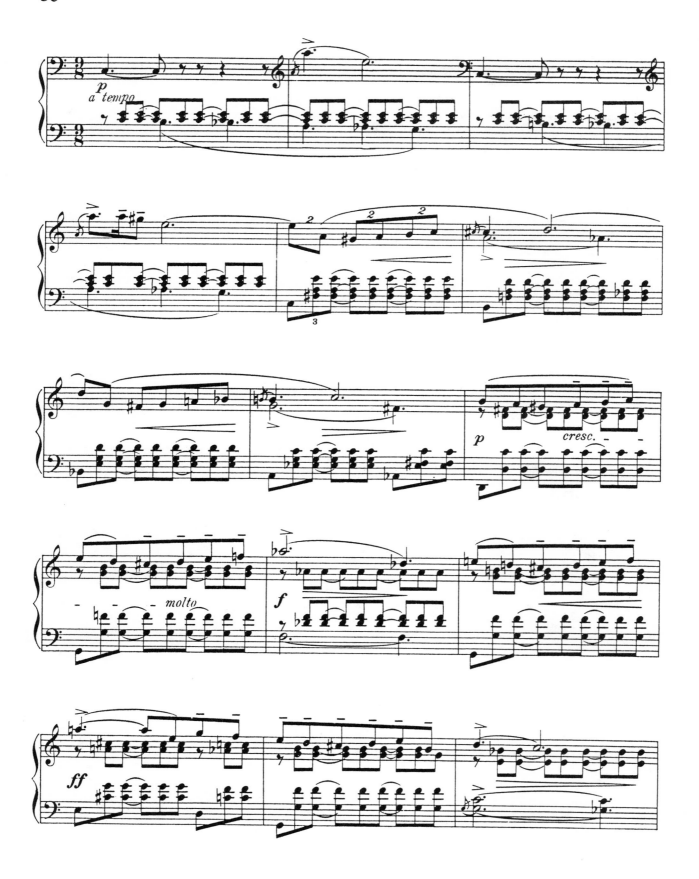

Anitra's Dance

(From incidental music to the play *Peer Gynt*, Op. 23, 1874–5)

Edvard Grieg

Tempo di Mazurka

In the Hall of the Mountain King

(From incidental music to the play *Peer Gynt*, Op. 23, 1874–5)

Edvard Grieg

Hornpipe in E Minor

George Frideric Handel
(Germany & England, 1685–1759)

Sarabande in D Minor

(From *Suite in D Minor*, published 1720)

George Frideric Handel

Largo

(Arranged from the opera *Xerxes*, 1738)

George Frideric Handel

Sonata No. 37 in D Major

(1st Movement) (before 1780)

Joseph Haydn
(Austria, 1732–1809)

Hungarian ["Gypsy"] Rondo

(Arrangement of the Finale of *Piano Trio in G Major*,
Hob.XV: No. 25, before 1795)

Joseph Haydn

Minore I

Maggiore

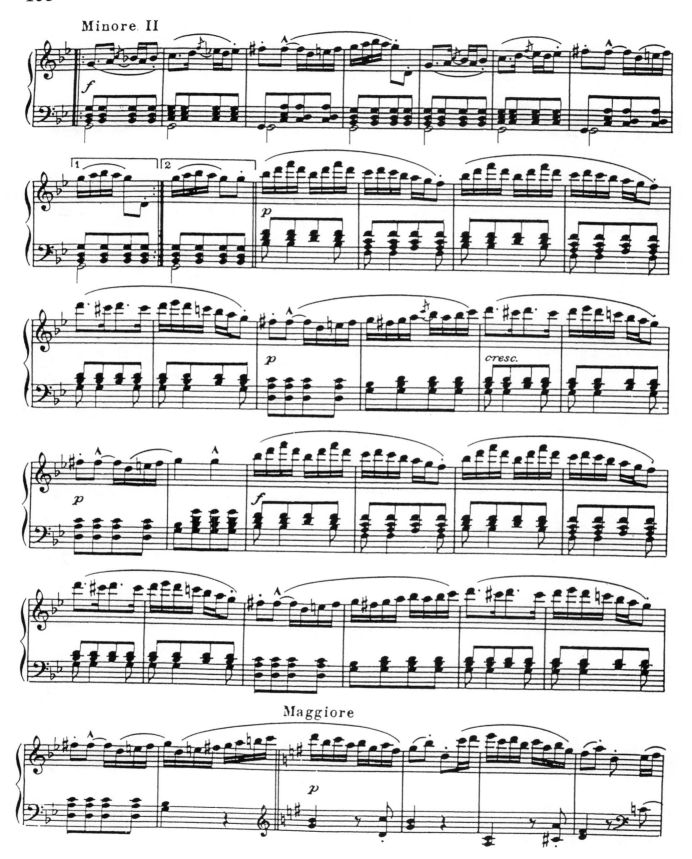

The Entertainer
A Rag Time Two Step (1902)

Scott Joplin
(United States, 1868–1917)

Maple Leaf Rag
(1899)

Scott Joplin

Tempo di marcia

Consolation No. 3 in D-flat Major

(From six *Consolations*, 1849–50)

Franz Liszt
(Hungary & Germany, 1811–1886)

Liebestraum No. 3 in A-flat Major

(Transcribed by the composer, *ca.* 1850,
from the last of the songs *Liebestraüme, 3 Notturnos*)

Franz Liszt

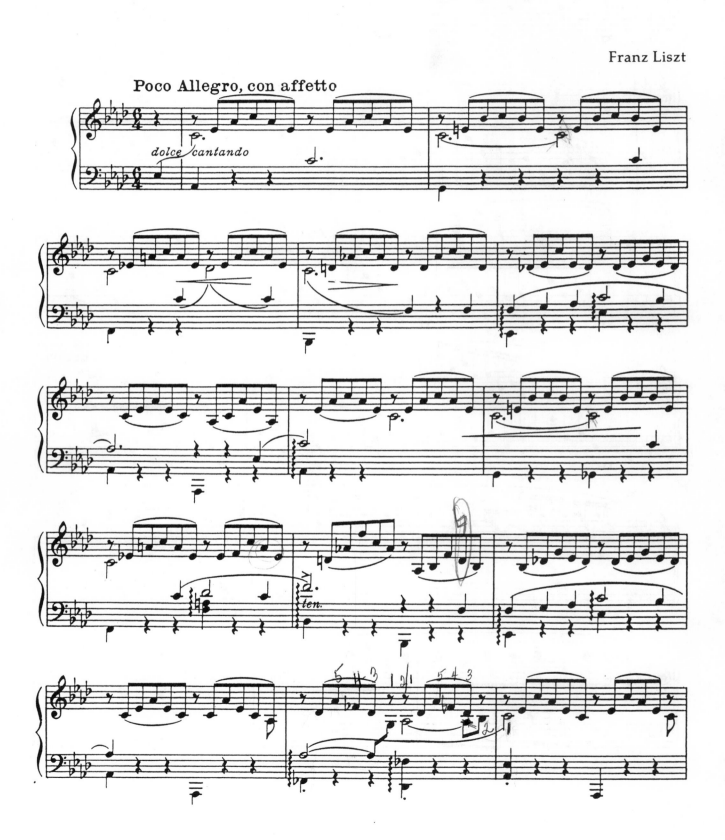

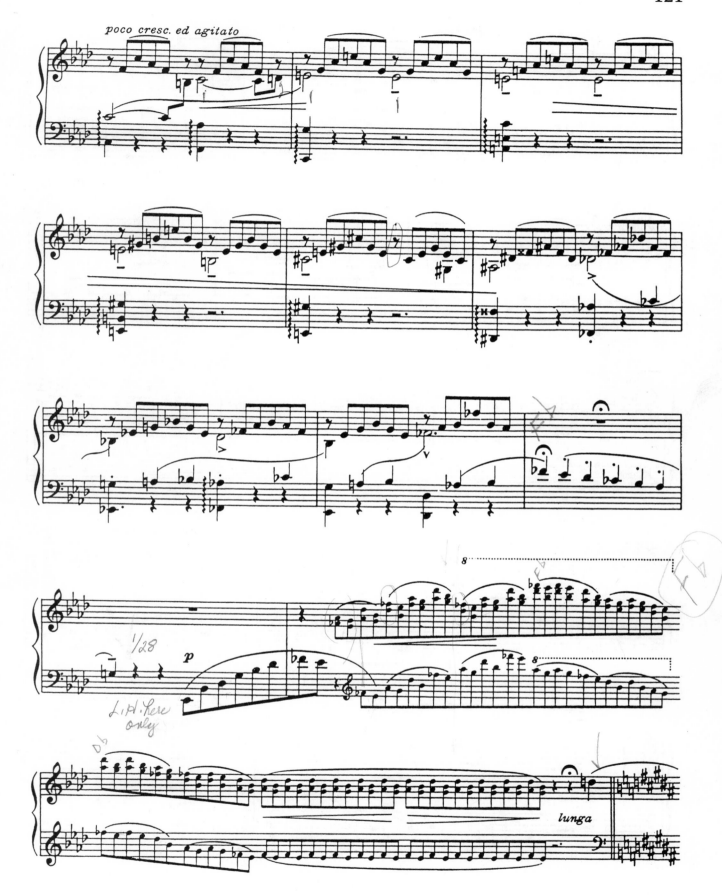

To a Wild Rose
Op. 51, No. 1
(From *Woodland Sketches*, 1896)

Edward MacDowell
(United States, 1860–1908)

With simple tenderness

slightly marked

Élégie

Op. 10, No. 5

("Mélodie" from *Ten Characteristic Pieces*, 1866)

Jules Massenet
(France, 1842–1912)

Venetian Gondola Song
Op. 30, No. 6
(From *Songs without Words*, 1833)

Felix Mendelssohn
(Germany, 1809–1847)

Spring Song

Op. 62, No. 6

(From *Songs without Words*, 1842)

Allegretto grazioso

Felix Mendelssohn

Spinning Song
Op. 67, No. 4
(From *Songs without Words*, 1845)

Felix Mendelssohn

138

Turkish Rondo

(Finale of Sonata No. 11 in A Major, K331, 1781–3)

Wolfgang Amadeus Mozart
(Austria, 1756–1791)

Two Early Minuets

K2 & K4 (1762)

Minuet in F Major [I]

Wolfgang Amadeus Mozart

Minuet in F Major [II]

Sonata No. 15 in C Major

K545 (1788)

I.

Wolfgang Amadeus Mozart

II.

RONDO
Allegretto

Promenade & The Old Castle

(From *Pictures at an Exhibition*, 1874)

Modest Petrovich Mussorgsky
(Russia, 1839–1881)

[Promenade I]

Moderato commodo assai e con delicatezza

ritard.

dimin.   *pp*

attacca

The Old Castle

[Promenade II]

Moderato non tanto, pesamente

[In the original, leads directly
to section 3: "Tuileries"]

Narcissus
Op. 13, No. 4
(From *Water Scenes*, 1891)

Ethelbert Nevin
(United States, 1862–1901)

Barcarolle

(From the opera *The Tales of Hoffmann*, publ. posth.)

Jacques Offenbach [Isaac Eberst]
(Germany & France, 1819–1880)

Menuet à l'Antique
Op. 14, No. 1
(From *Humoresques de Concert*, 1887)

Ignacy Jan Paderewski
(Poland, 1860–1941)

con forza la melodia

Prelude in C-sharp Minor

Op. 3, No. 2

(From *Fantasy Pieces*, 1893)

Serge Rachmaninoff
(Russia & United States, 1873–1943)

Minuet in A Minor

(From *First Book of Harpsichord Pieces*, 1706)

Jean-Philippe Rameau
(France, 1683–1764)

Tambourin*

(From *Harpsichord Pieces*, 1724)

Jean-Philippe Rameau

*a long, narrow drum from Provence

Pavane for a Dead Princess
(1899)

Maurice Ravel
(France, 1875–1937)

1er Mouvement

très doux et très lié

pp

Très grave

pp

p

Très grave

Romance

Op. 44, No. 1

(From the suite *Evenings in St. Petersburg,* 1860)

Anton Rubinstein
(Russia, 1829–1894)

The Swan

(Arranged from the orchestral suite
The Carnival of the Animals, 1886)

Camille Saint-Saëns
(France, 1835–1921)

First Gymnopédie*

(From *Three Gymnopédies*, 1888)

Erik Satie
(France, 1866–1925)

*1ST GYMNOPAIDIKE [Spartan dance of naked youths and men]. Slow and sorrowful.

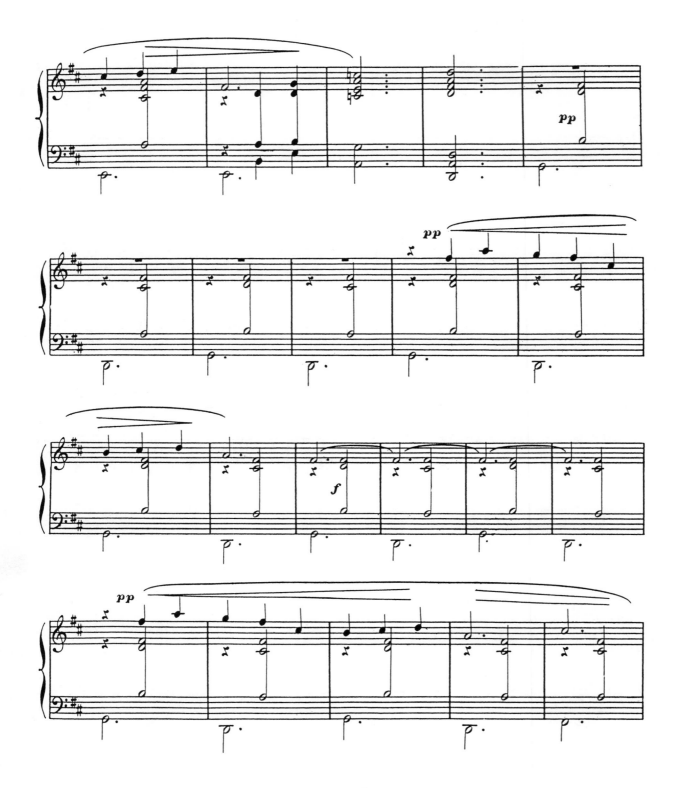

Sonata in D Major

(Balletto)

Longo 329 (date uncertain)

Domenico Scarlatti
(Italy, 1685–1757)

Non presto, ma a tempo di ballo

Pastorale in D Minor

Longo 413 (date uncertain)

Domenico Scarlatti

Serenade

(Transcribed from the song "Ständchen,"
from the cycle *Schwanengesang*, 1828)

Franz Schubert
(Austria, 1797–1828)

to

Moment Musical
Op. 94, No. 3
(From *Six Moments Musicaux, ca. 1823*)

Franz Schubert

Allegro moderato

Marche Militaire
Op. 51, No. 1
(From three *Marches Militaires, ca.* 1822,
arranged from the original for piano four-hands)

Franz Schubert

TRIO

Marcia D.C.

Träumerei

[Reverie] Op. 15, No. 7

(From *Scenes from Childhood,* 1838)

Robert Schumann
(Germany, 1810–1856)

Moderato

Child Falling Asleep
Op. 15, No. 12
(From *Scenes from Childhood*, 1838)

Robert Schumann

Important Event
Op. 15, No. 6
(From *Scenes from Childhood*, 1838)

Robert Schumann

The Happy Farmer

Op. 68, No. 10

(From *Album for the Young*, 1848)

Robert Schumann

Frisch und munter *(bright and gay)*

Etude in C-sharp Minor

Op. 2, No. 1

(From *Three Pieces*, 1887)

Alexander Scriabin
(Russia, 1872–1915)

Andante

Désir

[Desire] Op. 57, No. 1

(From *Two Pieces*, 1907)

Alexander Scriabin

Rustle of Spring
Op. 32, No. 3
(From *Six Pieces*, 1896)

Christian Sinding
(Norway, 1856–1941)

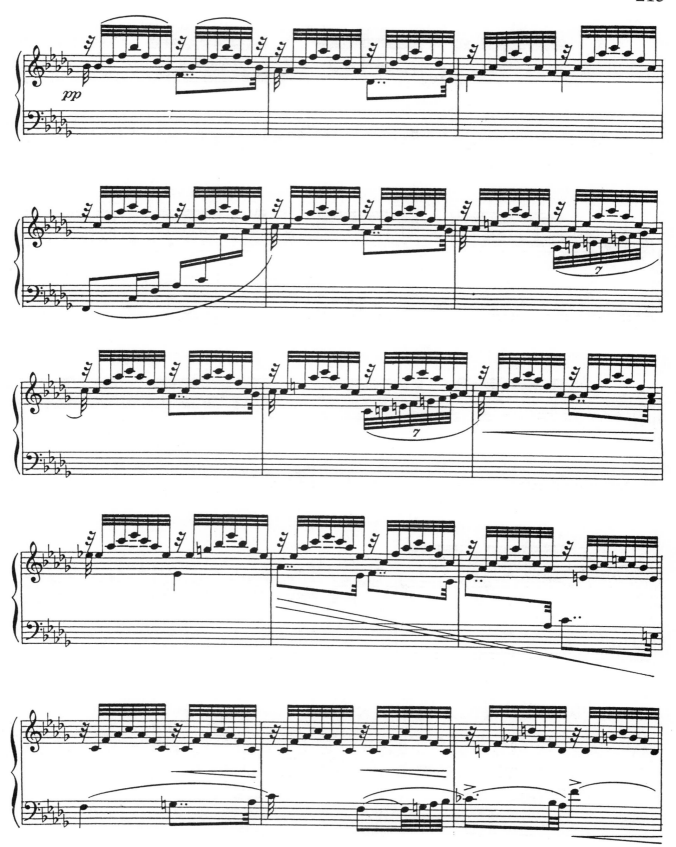

Memory of Bohemia
in the Form of a Polka

Op. 13, No. 1

(From two polkas, 1859–60)

Bedřich Smetana
(Czechoslovakia, 1824–1884)

On the Beautiful Blue Danube

Op. 314 (1867)

Johann Strauss Jr.
(Austria, 1825–1899)

Waltz

1.

Dal Segno senza repetisione al Fine.

Chanson Triste

[Sad Song] Op. 40, No. 2

(From *Twelve Pieces*, 1878)

Peter Ilyitch Tchaikovsky
(Russia, 1840–1893)

Waltz in E-flat Major

Op. 39, No. 9

(From *Album for the Young*, 1878)

Peter Ilyitch Tchaikovsky

Polka

Op. 39, No. 10

(From *Album for the Young*, 1878)

Peter Ilyitch Tchaikovsky